MEDITATIONS

SELECTED & ILLUSTRATED BY

PETER MAX

McGRAW-HILL BOOK COMPANY
New York   St. Louis   San Francisco   Düsseldorf
London   Mexico   Sydney   Toronto

Parts of the material in this book have been previously published by
Publisher's Hall Syndicate, Inc.

123456789HAHO798765432

Library of Congress Cataloging in Publication Data

Max, Peter, date
  Meditations.

    1. Meditations—Pictorial works. I. Title.
BV4832.2.M35   248'.3'0222   72-5874
ISBN 0-07-040990-0

INTRODUCTION

ENLIGHTENMENT IS MAN'S ONLY AND ULTIMATE GOAL. MANY GREAT SAGES AND SAINTS, PHILOSOPHERS, WANDERING MONKS AND SCIENTISTS HAVE GUIDED US THROUGH HISTORY WITH THEIR WORDS OF WISDOM, HOPING TO ENLIGHTEN US TO A PATH LEADING TO THE SUPREME GOAL OF LIFE.

IT IS THESE GREAT SAGES AND SAINTS THAT HAVE LED THE WAY FOR MANKIND IN BRINGING IN THE NEW AGE.

WE ARE ON THE THRESHOLD OF THE NEW AGE RIGHT NOW AND IT IS IN TIMES LIKE THESE THAT THE SPIRITUAL POWER OF GOD WILL MANIFEST ITSELF IN MANY WAYS.

I HOPE THAT THIS BOOK WILL FURTHER ENLIGHTEN READERS TOWARD THE GOLDEN PATH.

THIS BOOK IS DEDICATED TO —
YOGIRAJ SRI SWAMI SATCHIDANANDA
WHO HAS GUIDED ME WITH LOVE AND
WISDOM —

ATMAN
(PETER MAX)

WITH SPECIAL THANKS TO ALL THOSE WHO HAVE SENT
ME QUOTES, WHICH I HAVE USED VERBATIM.

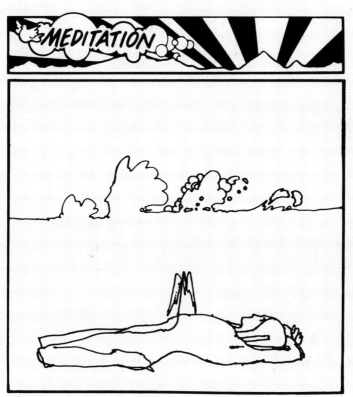

"Man must evolve for all human conflict a method which rejects revenge, aggression, and retaliation. The foundation of such a method is love."

Martin Luther King, Jr.

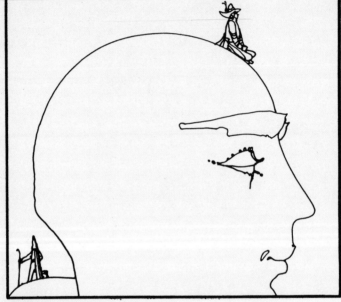

"Truth has no special time of its own. Its hour is now—always."

Albert Schweitzer

"We only need to fill each moment with experiencing and using and it ceases to burn."

Martin Buber

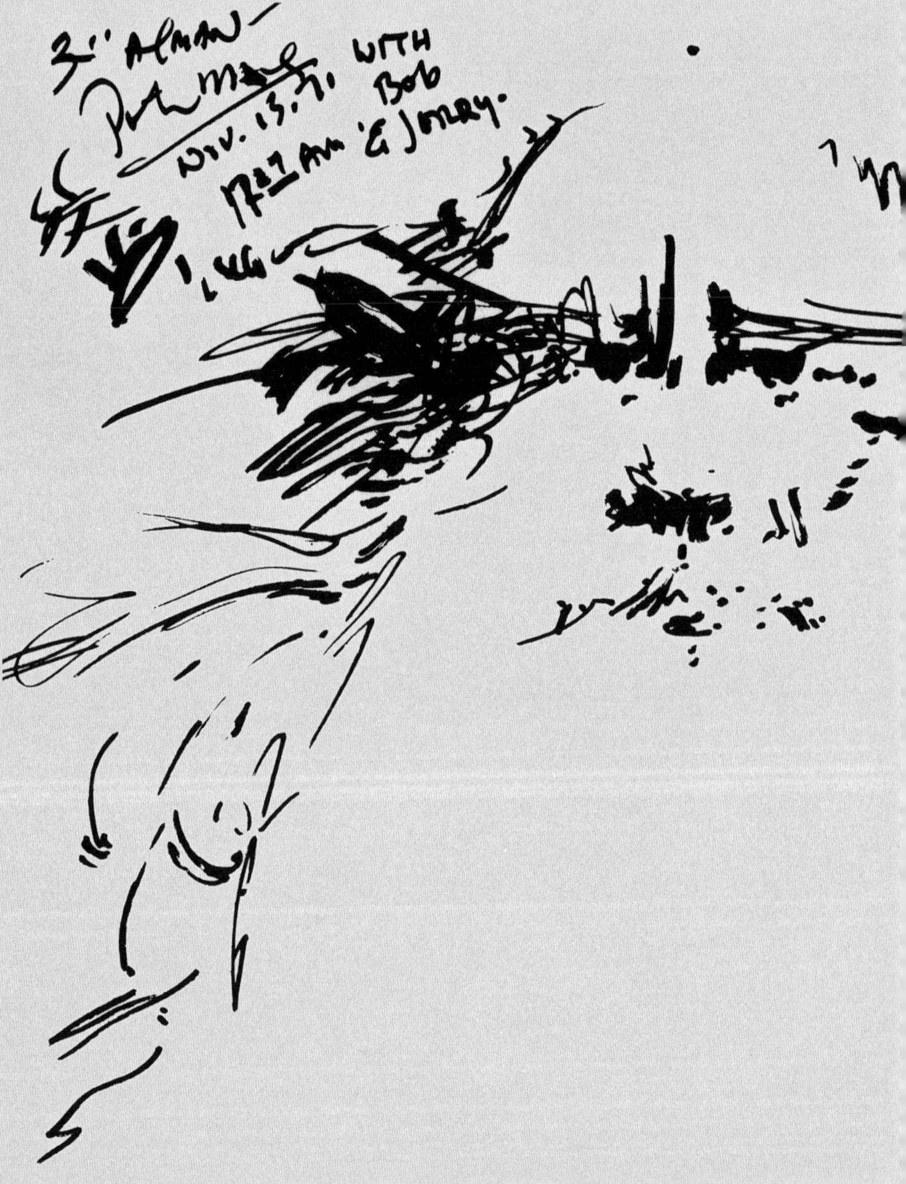
WITH
BOB
NOV. 13. 71
JERRY.

DALLAS -28.

"Your duty—your reward—your destiny is in the present moment."

Dag Hammarskjöld

"Life was meant to be lived, not understood."

Santayana

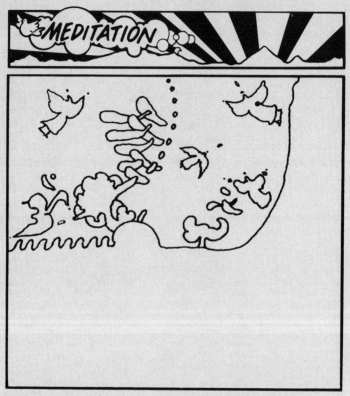

MEDITATION

"Birth is inevitable to what is dead and death is inevitable to what is born. This is the law of nature. Therefore you should not grieve."

Bhagavad Gita

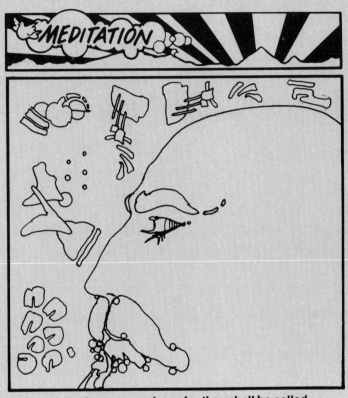

"Blessed are the peacemakers; for they shall be called the children of God."

Matthew V, 9

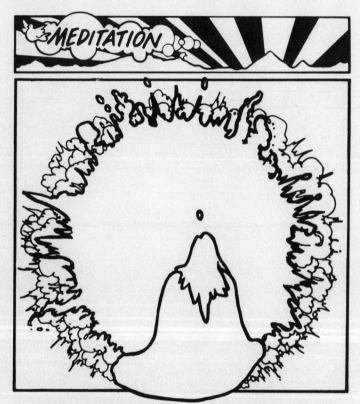

"What the superior man seeks is in himself. What the mean man seeks is in others."

Confucius

"A happy life consists of tranquility of mind."

Cicero

"The journey of a thousand miles begins with one step."
Lao-Tzu

MEDITATION

"Today is the first day of the rest of your life."

Anonymous

"Love all, trust a few, do wrong to no one."

Shakespeare

"When you've seen beyond yourself, then you may find peace of mind is waiting there."

George Harrison

"Now never will leave! It is always here. Like a clear canvas, it awaits our painting."

Swami Satchidananda

"Wear your love like heaven."

Donovan

MEDITATION

"Living is loving."

Charlos Brunet

"Don't oppose forces; use them. God is a verb, not a noun."

R. Buckminster Fuller

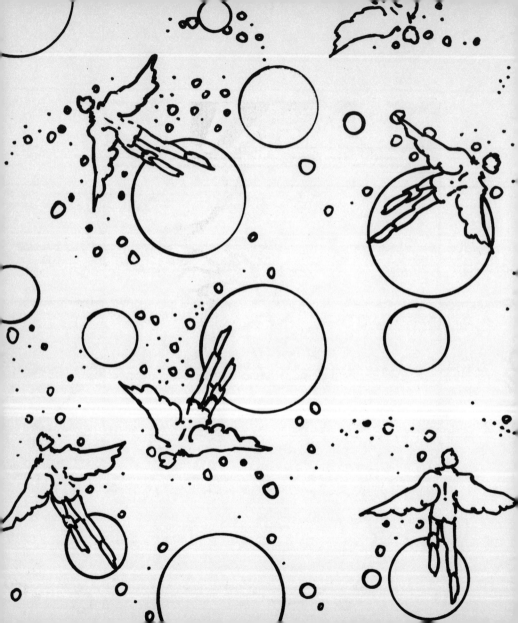

MEDITATION

"If you want to be happy, be."

Tennyson

"To draw, you must close your eyes and sing."

Pablo Picasso

"See not, touch not with your toes even, anything that is uncanny."

Vivekananda

"I make myself rich by making my wants few."

Thoreau

"The Earth is but one country; and mankind its citizens."

Baha'u'llah

"You and all men are here for the sake of other men."
R. Buckminster Fuller

"If we change the world, let us bear the mark of our intelligence."

Anonymous

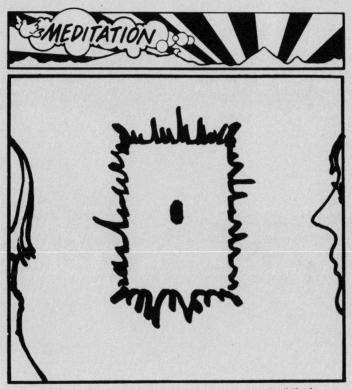

"Kindness is a language the deaf can hear and the blind can read."

Mark Twain

"Love neither judges nor condemns anyone."
Swami Satchidananda

"Joy is not in things; it is in us."

Wagner

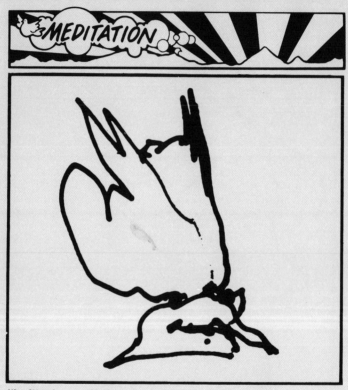

"I will take my life into my hands and I will use it."

Jimmy Webb

"Only that day dawns to which we are awake."

Thoreau

"Man is immortal because he has a soul, a spirit capable of compassion and sacrifice and endurance."

William Faulkner

"God made truth with many doors, to welcome every believer who knocks on them."

Kahlil Gibran

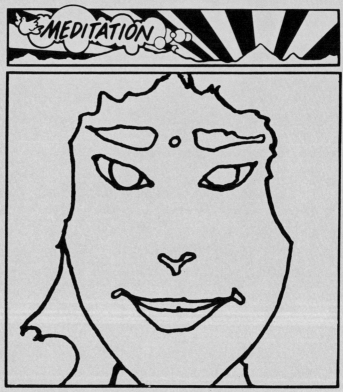

"The strongest man upon earth is he who stands most alone."

Henrik Ibsen

**"His daily prayer, far better understood
In acts than words, was simply doing good.**

Whittier

"The deeper that sorrow carves into your being, the more joy you can contain."

Kahlil Gibran

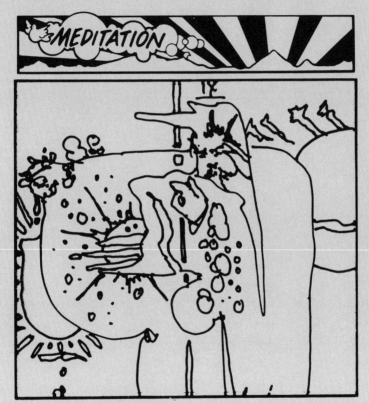

"What you would seem to be, be really."

Anonymous

"You don't live in a world all alone. Your brothers are here too."

Unknown

"All things change, nothing perishes."

Ovid

"The true value of a human being is determined primarily by the measure and the sense in which he has attained liberation from the self."

Albert Einstein

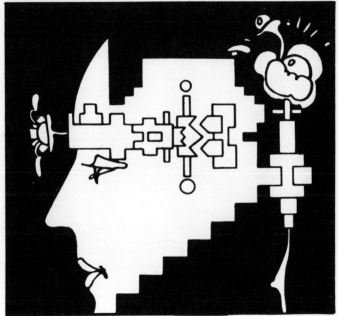

"Be not ashamed to say what you are not ashamed to think."

Montaigne

"Advice is like snow; the softer it falls, the longer it dwells upon, and the deeper it sinks into, the mind."

Samuel Taylor Coleridge

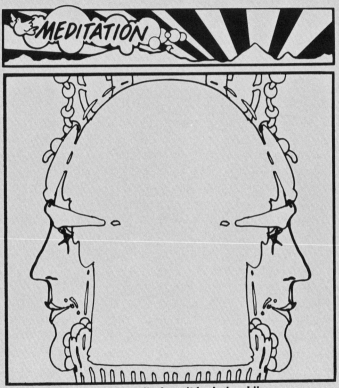

"He that won't be counselled can't be helped."
Benjamin Franklin

MEDITATION

"I was young and foolish then. Now I am older and foolisher."

Mark Twain

"To me old age is always 15 years older than I am."
Bernard M. Baruch

"All I know is that I know nothing..."

Emerson

MEDITATION

"Humor is the other side of tragedy.
Humor is a serious thing."

James Thurber

"All I really want to do, is, baby, be friends with you."
Bob Dylan

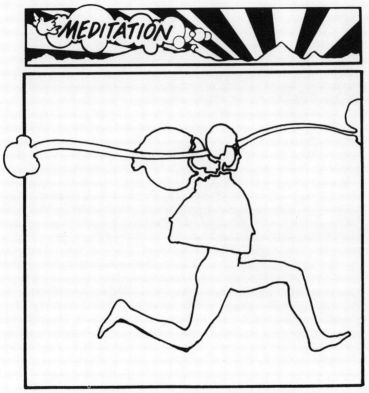

"Make no appointments, get no disappointments."
Swami Satchidananda

"It's fun to do the impossible."

Walt Disney

MEDITATION

"Heaven is exactly in the center of the chest of the man who has faith."

Salvador Dali

"An artist cannot speak about his art any more than a plant can discuss horticulture."

Jean Cocteau

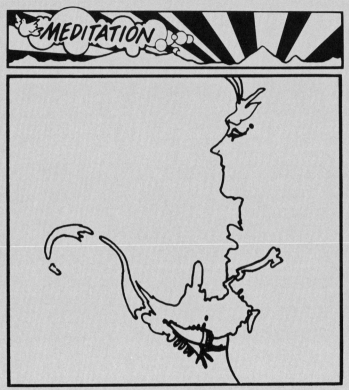

"Art is a lie that makes us realize the truth."

Pablo Picasso

MEDITATION

"A mind that is stretched by a new idea can never go back to its original dimensions."

Oliver Wendell Holmes

"Life is a matter of being born."

e.e. cummings

"Well: If 'I' am not speaking; If 'I' am not what 'I' thought 'I' was, how did 'I' get into this/Who am 'I'?"

Baba Ram Das

"Thought has form, shape, color, quality, substance, power, and weight."

Swami Satchidananda

"What you want, what you're hanging around in the world waiting for, is for something to occur to you."

Robert Frost

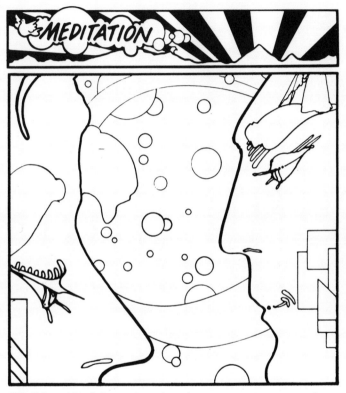

"Nothing astonishes men so much as common sense and plain dealing."

Emerson

"Those who know do not talk and talkers do not know."
Tao Te Ching

**"What is soul? It is like electricity—we don't really know
what it is, but it's a force that can light a room."**

Ray Charles

MEDITATION

"Life is fragile—handle with prayer."

Anonymous

MEDITATION

"To be alive at all involves some risk."

Harold MacMillan

"I feel that the capacity to care is that which gives life its deepest significance."

Anonymous

"Youth is the time for the adventures of the body, but age for the triumphs of the mind."

Logan Pearsall Smith

MEDITATION

"Every man's life is a fairy tale written by God's fingers."

Hans Christian Andersen

"A Man who has exercised his mind to the utmost, knows his nature. Knowing his nature, he knows heaven."

Mencius

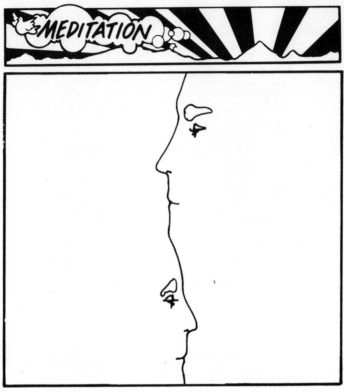

"As soon as you trust yourself, you will know how to live."

Goethe

"All evil vanishes from life for him who keeps the sun in his heart."

Rama Yama

"Let him that would move the world, first move himself."
Socrates

"Reverence for life ... from ants to men, it is developing a sense of oneness with all life."

Albert Schweitzer

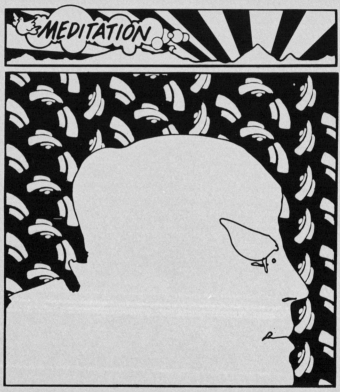

"You gain strength, courage and confidence by every experience in which you really stop to look fear in the face."

Eleanor Roosevelt

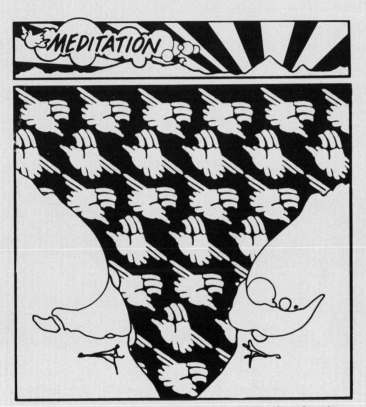

"Of a truth, men are mystically united, a mysterious bond of brotherhood makes all men one."

Carlyle

"Nothing is lost by peace; everything may be lost by war."
Pope Paul VI

"There is only one God and nothing else besides."

Old Testament

"Ask and it shall be given to you, seek and ye shall find, knock and it shall be open unto you."

Jesus

"Seek ye good not evil that ye may live."

Amos V,14

"God cannot be realized if there is the slightest attachment to the things of the world. A thread cannot pass through the eye of a needle if the tiniest fibre sticks out."

Guru Nanak

MEDITATION

"My friend shall forever be my friend, and reflect a ray of God to me."

Thoreau

"Grief can take care of itself, but to get full value of joy, you must have somebody to divide it with."

Mark Twain

"Joy and serenity are within man, not outside him."

Chekov

"Worry is like a rocking chair, it goes back and forth but gets you nowhere."

Mark Twain

"There is nothing either good or bad   but thinking makes it so."

Shakespeare

MEDITATION

"A man's mouth speaks what his heart is full of."

the Bible

"The Lord can never be established nor created; the
formless One is limitlessly complete in Himself."

Guru Nanak

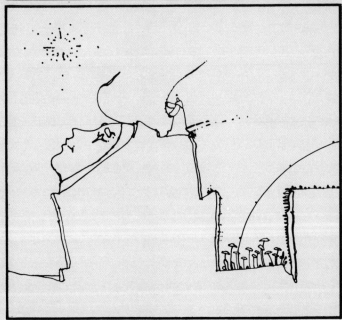

"You must love life, for life is God and to love life is to love God."

Leo Tolstoy

"How does the meadowflower its bloom unfold?
Because the lovely little flower is free
Down to its root, and in that freedom bold."

Wordsworth

"Give light, and darkness will disappear of itself."

Erasmus

"The great use of life is to use it for something that outlasts it."

William James

MEDITATION

"A man that is young in years may be old in hours, if he have lost no time."

Francis Bacon

"Peace can not be kept by force; it can only be achieved by understanding."

Albert Einstein

"I am me, but part of you."

Unknown

"I love you not only for what you are, but for what I am when I am with you."

Unknown

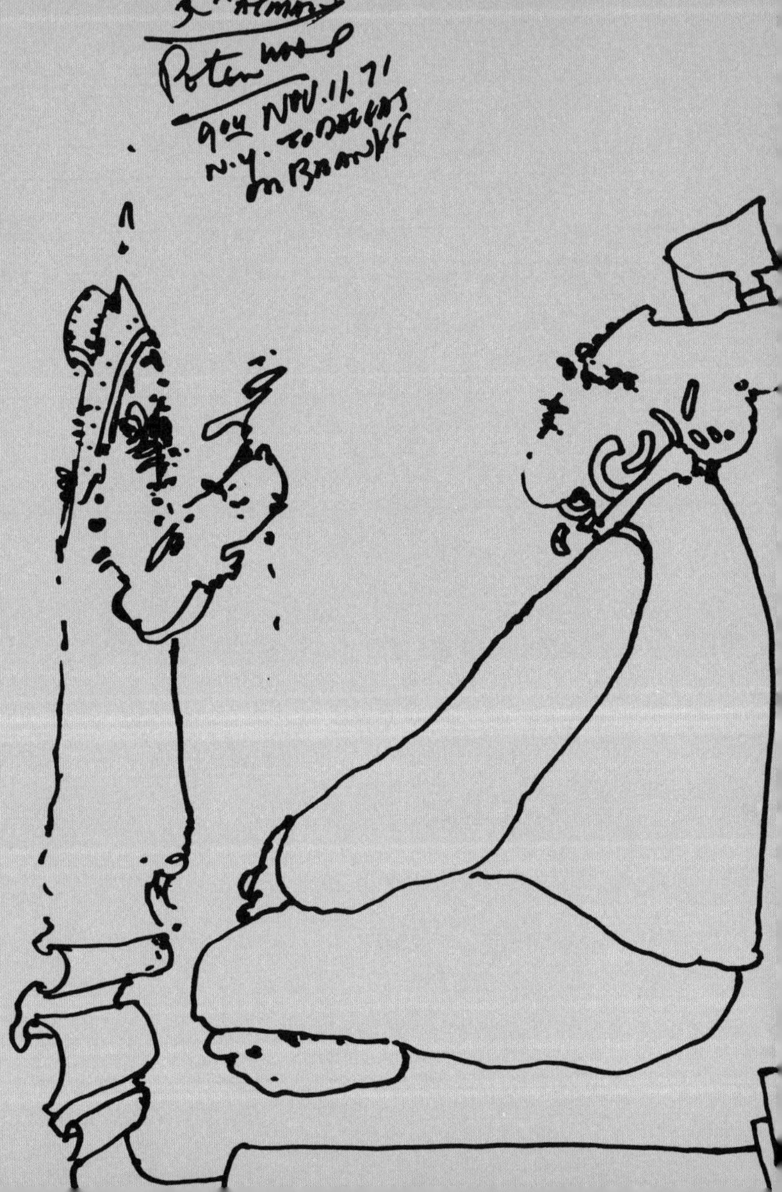
9:04 NOV. 11. 71
N.Y. TO DALLAS
ON BRANIFF

"Though I am different from you, we were born involved in one another."

T'ao Ch'ien

"... to thine own self be true,
   And it must follow, as the night the day
   Thou canst not then be false to any man."

Shakespeare

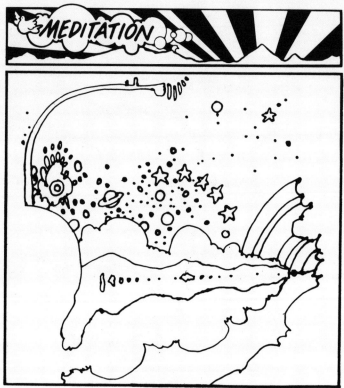

"Never does nature say one thing and wisdom another."
Juvenal

"The infinite Goodness has such wide arms that it takes whatever turns to it."

Dante

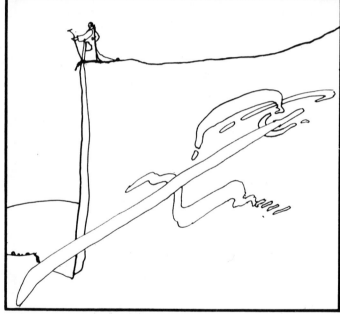

"In the midst of winter I finally learned that there was in me an invincible summer."

Albert Camus

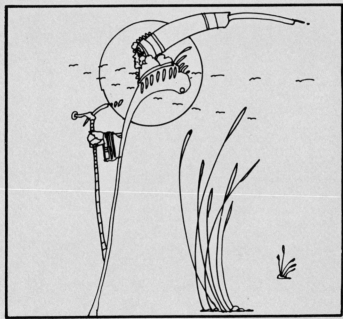

"There is no joy but calm."

Thoreau

"My sweet Lord, I really want to see you. I really want to be with you."

George Harrison

"And in the end the love we take is equal to the love we make."

Beatles

"There may be more beautiful times: but this one is ours."

Sartre

"Love released is love fulfilled."

Unknown